Winner, 2009 CAKETRAIN CHAPBOOK COMPETITION

MICHAEL BURKARD, *Final Judge*

GHOST MACHINE BY BEN MIROV

[a journal and press]

CAKETRAIN
[a journal and press]

Box 82588, Pittsburgh, Pennsylvania 15218

www.caketrain.org

Printed in the United States of America.

ISBN 978-0-988-89150-0

for C

The ghosts the poems were written for are the ghosts of the poems. We have it second-hand. They cannot hear the noise they have been making.

—Jack Spicer

GHOST OF A MORNING
AFTER YOU LEFT ME

I hover in front of a chain link fence for hours reading signs. My day is a long protracted silence. I pour myself into a phone call to avoid a little rain. Wind comes through a crack in the glass. They put new lights in the basilica months ago, I didn't notice. I program a future version of myself to remember a face slick with seawater, ringed with wet hair. The message is sent back with nothing inside. I can't believe my life was like this three years ago. I would have sex and just lie there, thinking about things I had to do. I woke up in a grocery store. I was buying broccoli.

GHOST RECEPTOR

The knowledge of my receivers grows dim.
I can only misquote what the voice tries to say.
I put it down in little marks.
I tell Meric it makes me sad.
I tell Dan I'm wiser now.
My head is full of *Love Is Chemicals*.
I'm sleeping on a couch.

GHOST LIFE

I'm living in a dream where a woman has a blurry face. Other people consider themselves Warriors fans. I look at a plastic bottle. I try to get more references. My new place will have hardwood floors. I'll boil Tom some water. I can't tell the portal what's on my mind. I talk with my mom about what's getting me down. I change *love poem* to *move pole*. I take BART to Oakland. I think of others as dots.

SPACECASE

I come to a rain condenser in the shape of Erin. It's almost dark
outside. I can't stand taking naps too late. Is this how literary
characters escape? Friends fall through my poems in search of
new life. We go to the roof and put a blanket on Victor. I search
his head for something to do. I remember how to carry a snare
drum. Logan gets a stamp on my inner-right wrist. I can't sit
still or eat my lamb.

SAME GHOST

I walk through love with a mannequin's arm. Things are the
same as they were two weeks ago. It's a cool idea to have the
woman eat the man made of dreams. I act like myself at a coffee
shop and try not to shake. My bed is an ear that cannot record.
I can't hear the voice that shifts through the barriers. She pukes
in my shower and falls asleep. I switch *cheesesteak* for *burrito*
and feel the same. Her boyfriend's name is something else.

GHOST OF ONE SUMMER NIGHT

Thanks for coming to 12 Galaxies.

I'm not calling the Vampire anymore.

I can't keep thinking of August.

You don't have to drink about the boat.

You don't have to take off your pants.

Sorry about the boots on your bed.

I just want a job with an income.

I go down on the breeze.

The earlobe is wet.

NAMELESS GHOST

Validation comes on the dance floor in waves.

I see them through a lens high above.

I imagine a woman in a room with Fleetwood Mac.

I read the email to see what she saw.

I do it to kill time and nothing else.

At 4 AM you must exist.

GHOST (1:42 AM)

My ideas are boring. She bleeds on the sheets. The wind blows over pavement and into an ear. If you park on Valencia, you may get a ticket. I erase her from the poem about the park. There are fifteen pages left in the life experience. Is this a good place to sleep? The spirit world shifts behind me. There's coffee on my shirt, not blood. I can't absorb information on a bench in Dolores. I had a dream we were in a hotel. Your blonde friend was faceless. She offered me salsa.

I spend all day looking at other people's writing. Is this a blithe
gash that was intended? I grab a case of Bud. He hits me in the
head and I turn around. I see *Taquiera* in red neon. Flying over
the city, Jared lets me steer. I can't try on jackets anymore.
Even though I know she's not the one, I think of us on a bike.
I can't catch Joseph and Bella jumps on my back and this means
something. I cut up missionary pamphlets to make a collage.
Waiting in the morning for my hair to look right, I feel like shit.
My work is an obvious cloud. Every door in the cloud is locked.
Eating with the kids, I tell them nothing about my life. Later, a
man named Malcolm calls.

FILLMORE GHOST

I arrive late and I don't buy a drink. I keep my hands in my
pockets and bob. I look around for strangers. Some lights are on.
Some are flickering. Andy tells me about his surfing trip and I
wince. There are no thoughts anywhere. She arrives and I can't
remember her name and she kisses me. The last three songs
are dim. I can't find an ATM. I throw the poster in the trash.
My pants are covered in beer.

We work in a room with the blinds down. You can eat pizza all the time. I remember swimming in the ocean with her. I pass a yellow cable over the coffee. Two weeks and she touched me there. Crossing the Bay is thinking time. Cigarettes are tiny men, not women. I bet you're cold. We make out against some graffiti. Poems can't be typed. Other times, I wonder what he's like in bed. I buy noodles at midnight. Couples on the street piss me off, then make me happy. What's your trick for going to sleep?

DOLORES PARK GHOST

We have plans to meet in a shadow.

We sit in the park for an hour.

Someone hands me their homework.

A little hand grabs my throat.

My kids fall asleep in dirty t-shirts.

I'm sorry about your crush.

I'm smashed after three drinks.

GHOST CHAPTER

I replace *Hot Lesbian Sandwich* with *Elements Taken from Trees*.

My shoes are somewhere beneath the couch.

I push my face into a memory.

I dream of *Where Is Juan Gris* in a pipe-filled room.

I think of myself in a different city.

I'm wearing a blue hoodie.

My hair falls in my eyes in a fashionable way.

I begin to write *after the wave.*

SAN FRANCISCO OVER CLOUDS

I stand on a roof that doesn't belong to me. I write three letters
to her in my head. I get nervous about dating. My unborn sister
should hand me the key. Leah calls and giant moths fly around
in a book. One stands to the side with gold chains on his neck.
Dan keeps my mind in a wet towel. I wish I could get the cube
off my chest. The best way to proceed is to disconnect. I can't
finish my aloo palak. I fill my drinks with hands. I promise to
be a wedding date.

SLEEPLESS NIGHT GHOST

I go to a shop where they sell machines that keep you up.
People flow in and out of the infrastructure like haywire birds.
It doesn't matter what I say to the recording device. Nothing
can save the face blowing across the face. Someone catches me
and shoves enough wire through my dream. Someone getting
out of bed to the sound of someone showering. Someone eating
pieces in the dark. It scares me through another night with no
ideas. I need artificial clouds to give. If we are ever in a car
together, I hope light pours through the windshield. I plan to
be another language in the body of a deer.

.

EYE, GHOST

Eye wake up in a construct. Eye lay on my
bed and sweat. Eye replay final moments. Eye try to
picture her face. Eye program a future version of myself
to remember it, slick with seawater, ringed with wet hair.
Eye go to a little shop where they sell machines
that keep you up. Eye lay the crumpled body next
to a convenience store. Eye place the organs in separate
aluminum trays. Eye stand on the street like every car
belongs to her. Eye Know. It doesn't matter what Eye
say to the recording device. Nothing can save the face

blowing across the face. Eye drink too much before the
game. Eye can't walk to the end of the block.
Eye turn around and hear a voice. Eye smash my
face into a neck. Eye try to sleep there for
a night. Eye never open the envelope marked C. Eye
wonder what he's like in bed. Eye erase her from
the poem about the dark. Eye stretch my arm through
brainwork's shadowy circuits. Eye bum around on couches for a
month. Eye tell them nothing about my life. Eye hear
the words outside at night. Eye plan to be another

shadow in the body of a deer. Eye come out
of BART with headphones and no memory. Eye wake up
in a grocery store. Eye wander to a map. Eye
wander through the rain. In my dreams, Eye have the
same problems. Eye live in an empty carcass. Eye work
in a cloud. Eye can't slow down the shadow process.
Eye can't go to sleep. Eye go down on the
breeze. The breeze is wet. Eye taste sea urchin and
spit. Eye can never touch the same breast twice. Eye
can never revisit our forest. Eye touch a night machine

in the shape of a woman. She can only stay
for a moment. Eye put her face inside a bed.
She sucks my nipple while Eye sleep. Eye see the
dead part in everything, shining and dull. Its hands are
raised like it's begging for food. It gives me my
third drink for free. Eye erase her from the poem
about the park. Eye can't cope with waves that help
me sleep. Eye have cruel dreams. Eye buy noodles at
midnight. Eye arrive at a bar like one who can
mimic. Eye pause in the mirror. Eye make things up

to disappear. She spends too long talking and Eye get
lonely. My brains are dripping on a wood bench. Eye
say *green bunnies* to protect us from the silence we
make. There are glass windows all around love. Eye tell
her nothing about my life. Eye feel like sex with
an android on television. Eye beat the shit out of
the steering wheel. Eye think of others washing their hands
in a cold dark beam. Eye can't decipher the code.
It was written on a napkin. Eye touch my hard-on.
Eye step back outside. Eye hear the voice that shifts

through the barriers. Eye feel wrecked by a bunch of
faces. Eye can't deal with ambiguous nocturnes. Eye speak to
a skull inside the breeze. Eye don't see the current
that carries me there. Eye walk through love with a
mannequin's arm. Eye look for a plan to cipher my
life. Eye promise myself to never return. Eye drink Old
English in the kitchen with some crackers. Eye see a
floating head. Eye take huge leaps to a garage full
of weapons. Eye can't sit still or eat my lamb.
Eye contain computers and a desk. Eye intend to become

myself. Eye hover in front of a chain-link fence for
hours reading signs. Eye finish my paperwork and crash. Eye
have dead bird. Eye learn to restrain and think about
years. Eye empty ideas into a tube. Eye forget ideas
in the shower. Eye can't find the *green bunny* poem.
Eye start to freak out. Eye live in a dump
with lots of light. Eye nod my head in silence.
Eye imagine our grandkids wearing nondescript masks. Eye lock the
door as fast as Eye can. Eye see her walking
through darkness and she says nothing. Eye approach her with

my daydream shatterer. Eye try to make a connection. Eye
receive a message from a blank stare. Eye can tell
when a relationship bends. It's the last thing to touch
the night. Eye kiss and kiss with one earphone. Eye
press *send* and feel sick. Eye can't remember her name.
Eye walk through a forest of empties. Eye fall asleep
on the floor. Eye pour myself into a phone call.
Eye avoid a night alone. Eye no longer run from
dream worms. Eye don't expect to see her for years.
Eye put on a clean t-shirt. Eye need artificial clouds

to live. Eye can't take off my face. Eye see
like three shows a week. Eye fall in love with
nothingness. Eye lose all of my echoes to friends. Eye
fall in love with patches of skin. Eye don't expect
a reply. Eye spend the day on the couch. Eye
have dead feelings. They float through the air. They touch
the nodes outside at night. Eye can't believe my life
was like this a year ago. Eye would lie there
thinking of things Eye had to do. Eye woke up
in a construct. Eye was buying coffee. Eye remember being

in the ocean with her. Eye probably won't see her
for years. Eye watch the rain through a window. Eye
construct little machines to pass the time. They keep me
awake at night. They float on the currents that move
to the edge. That's what they're for. Eye send them
away. Eye never said what Eye meant to say. Eye
can never revisit a moment. Eye can't shut down the
recording device. Eye touch a face made of glass. The
nothing that builds itself while Eye sleep. Eye smash the
construct to remember its ghost. Eye never reach the edge

I don't know if a salve was applied or what. I crawl through the crevice and panic. I come upon an egg and wolf it down. Who was chasing me through the brush? He's staring at neon graffiti and doesn't look away. He looks like a rich kid on acid. He turns into a duffle bag. The man I have sex with is me. I don't dream about you. I find your feelings' cloud. It doesn't end with Brian and Jeremy at Delirium. It's better without music in the dark. If I could, I would check your text. No one drinks Tanqueray with three rocks. *No More Bad Dreams* in kid writing with pink and yellow torn up pieces of paper. She'll love me when I have a book in my hand. I sit next to her and feel awkward. I didn't know about their files. Everyone should go upstairs. I don't wake up because I can't see you. I replay final moments. I step back inside. I never wrote what I meant to say. I can almost reach my keys. I'd like to kill a forty. I'm sorry about your year.

FOG MACHINE

I can write a poem a day when no one is looking. It gives me a power I describe as *flakes*. There are shadows in my head with breasts. Come see my "roof." We tell each other nothing about ourselves and go home happy. There's no point in coffee. I never come to this bar. She grows quiet and dances badly. Something pulls me to bed. People are waiting for me on the other side. My secret is house music. I intend to become myself. I drink too much beer before the game. My life shakes a little underwater. I will probably never take a train to Berkeley. I smash my face into her shoulder blade. I stretch my arm through brainwork's shadowy branches. She sucks my nipple while I sleep. They can only stay for a moment. I order tacos with rice and beans. Sentences fall out of Michelle. I can't cope with waves that help me sleep. Some of them are drinking wine. One of them hits the other in the face. I look at her ass and it makes me sad. I unlock two doors and give piggyback rides. I wait for a plan to cipher my life. A bus passes by and I don't forget. I see a floating head.

I am through love. Can cities grow in your stomach? When I write *this is yellow*, I step out of a tree. I become the street I am walking. I have two hours left. They say things to fill space and touch. I don't keep her pictures in envelopes marked *C*. These up the ante a bit by leaving off the human element. The iron weight of the mundane sounds drag. Chris and Leah come in the front. Part two begins after they sit down. The RLS kicks in and doubt. I'm not calling what's-her-name. As long as we're on the same network, I have dead words. I find information. A shape falls at the feet of 12:22. I've been up for hours with a glass. Heard Alberto almost stabbed you with a pen. There's nothing better than a siphoning alone. I talk in little blinks to strangers. Days go faster as I see rain. Human samples scan the street. The program is writing files. Maybe this sentence is better. Fourteen minutes left.

UMMM MACHINE

Nothing left of the dream on the hill leaves me feeling washed.
The sentence in my mind is *turn your breasts into cash with music*.
I lack organizational skills and love and calls over the infra-
structure. My soul is sent to another city to organize a puddle. I
hear the bullshit and choose another. I'm made of enemies and
steam and things you've done to me. Our relationship is
doomed. The claw comes and goes. I am a smoker. You are a
door to a switch. I am beginning to travel. I think about planes
and suitcases and what shampoo. They send back no reply. I
serve them waffles and say *say please*. J won't stop biting his
toes. I lost my crush. It has something to do with *cloud*. I've
been inside it or a while. I've lost all my echoes to friends. What
is it about your face? She tells me she has AIDS and then *just
kidding*. We have plans on the platform at nine. I don't expect
to see her for years. All of my kids are on freeze. C walks
through a memory of Dolores. Sometimes she is with me,
sometimes not. I can bum around on couches for a month. I
can buy shoes.

I can write this all day. Things go on and trees. I roll over my hard-on. It's cold and damp. We make out until I stop talking. Do you want my long drawn-out opinion? Not in love with it. Less *Lolita* and more *Shopgirl*. I don't know how I got my hands on it, but it was a waste of my time, for sure. Whatever it is, it's a plank. I don't fuck around with laces. It's time to think in small discreet packets. He looks at me like I care she's on his lap. Who folded the blankets? I barely understand Old English in the kitchen with some crackers. It makes her look dikey. This is why people come to the Mission. Can they drink? Can we be more uptight? Can we listen to New Order? I'm filtering down. It's the best movie I see all week. Next week is the boat. Please let him know I'm interested in all types of writing that might be called poetry. I need an intelligent woman to read a story. Why do I kill you? I feel the same way. The part about the horses and the poles is clichéd. I try to get published elsewhere.

TIME MACHINE

One thing leads to the next. I can't look at a tree without waking up. I don't even want to mention my X. Traces of twilight cling to my beard. I crave the attention of cloud machines. Why is *dream* better than *think*? I feel the exhaustion of the escalator. My waves go out and never return. My waves go out and never return. I step out my door and hear the sound of cars. The pain of the last one, unable to find me. The archer in the screen, the starlight in the spine. Further down Van Ness, a briefcase appears. My lungs are spelt *lings*. A ghost in my writing hand. The promise of nothing in my pen. What kind of university is this? A TV flickers in my heart. Snow-white my disintegrating voice. Bone-white my tablet of air. Next up, the fourth ventricle. And then, maybe *hydrophobia*. The wind in my hair, the rain in my eyes. The days tick by and go unnoticed. I can never touch the same breast twice. I can never revisit a forest.

I don't expect a reply. I wish I knew what email you were talking. She's probably watching him surf. No one has cars. Bosco and I make characters. It's eleven thousand words. I don't put my name on the poem. I learn to restrain and think about spit. We drink forties in Dolores. The reading was great. The jackets keep coming. They look at me like I'm matches. Mo drops three Parliaments. It's better on Wednesdays. They work in patterns and the patterns are leaves. Once shot, they become silent clouds. How can I miss paper cutouts? Many of them live in the East Bay. I saw them on Geary. She avoids a story altogether. I forget about two initials. I have to get this off my mind. His father made him wear a dress to school over vegetarian sandwiches. I want a relationship with noise. You two kill me with your *blaah*. Keep drinking water. We talk for five minutes. It's shaped like sleep.

I approach her with my daydream shatterer. I make things up to see my reflection. We walk together with her bike between us. I don't say anything about Saturday night. I wake up in a construct. The room is dark and filled with bobbing deads. Black t-shirts cover the music. I've lost the place she entered the forest. A blue car is parked by a pencil. A factory is making cubes. There is a long winding path that leads to a house. Behind the house there are triangular trees. I've been lying in bed all day with an empty. TV cures the way I think. The sky is designed to envelope anything but memory. I have to send her a letter with a mix. I'm a total slouch when it comes to rain. Gray lines echo through the light. Thoughts about women are balloons full of blood. I take a walk to buy a slice. Its hands are raised like it's begging for food. We meet at Dolores after the party. Bottle rockets burn my hands. Elena drags me down 20th past my old place. The Lone Palm is empty. Dan is still alive.

We go out for drinks and attack a dumpster. D takes off his pants and tries to have sex with J. My lighter is busted. I run to catch the 22. The next step is to think like Brian. D escapes through the kitchen. I forget to lock up the knives. Her drawer is full of strawberry condoms. I look for the *green bunny* poem. She drops me down the side. It's sober day. Thanks for coming to the show. I wish they were something else, not alone. Your emails wince. J calls me shitface with tears in his eyes. We meet at 8 and grab a bite to eat. Someone says my name is Booth. She gives me my third drink for free. Z laughs whenever a kid starts a fight. There isn't enough sex to go around. I can't believe they killed-off Bodie. I've decided to stop sleeping you. It's a bag of baseball bats I hand the kids. Most of the day is spent on the floor. I never open the envelope marked C. I walk down Valencia over a grate. The next step is to think like Brian.

I go to bars and don't know. I should be in Oakland looking for jokes. I can tell when a relationship bends. It's the last thing that happened. People begin to walk. There's no jacket for weather. Beneath everything is a conscious mind I'd like to play. Your email made me feel like I'm piling time. I wear a hoodie into the station. I come out of BART with headphones and memory. It's great to see them on the street and not go along. We back off the record label. No show at the Hemlock. I like what you've done with the lettering. I'm afraid to tell him little letters. I stand on the street like every car is her. I stumble around until I get home. I post a picture of the Silver Surfer. I'd rather no one saw. Every breeze is fixed. Every shadow touched. I am working with a friend to design the site. I hope I have managed to assuage your fears about the poems. It should be a fun thing for all of us. It should be done by now. Drew comes to get me and we go to a party where I talk to Ellen. Thanks, Cedar.

The next phase of my life begins. I can't plan
too far into the future. A kid named R takes
me on the tour. I hear screaming during the interview
but pretend not to notice. I don't think I'm qualified
to work with level twelve. You're on the peninsula today.
It's just a piece of paper. People in San Francisco
know this isn't real rain. R calls me a bitch
with tears in his eyes. E and I meet and
grab a bite to eat. It was great to know
you. I want you to meet my kids. M carries

a dead cup. T asks strangers for money. B gets
hit with a chair and looks up at a building
and feels left out at a bar. J assaults four
kids and two adults. R needs to be restrained. D
learns the code word and smiles. R wants to kill
me, or just fuck me up. A little black fist
hits my chest for no reason. I teach D how
to brush his teeth. I bring him toast with jam.
I walk out to the playground. I catch a pigeon
in a blanket while they scream. I should tell you

something about my life. I run to catch the twenty-two.
I'm in a meeting. I spend the day in eight
rooms. All my kids are on freeze. One dresses up
like a mermaid. Another paints his face like a female
vampire. R gets mad and throws a computer. I lock
him in a room. I teach him how to fold
a plane. Books fly out the window. Spit runs down
my cheek. D takes off his pants and simulates sex
with J. The next step is to think like B.
D escapes through the kitchen. I think you'd be proud

of my accomplishments. I forget to lock up the knives.
J follows me down the street with a blade. D
calls me a nigga on the bed. M pisses himself
and I help him shower. I put ketchup on his
hash browns. I hold A's legs while G and Z
pin his arms. I don't open the envelope marked C.
I come from the kitchen with toast. I wipe spit
off my face. My kids fall asleep in dirty t-shirts.
I don't wanna talk about work. I take the thirty-three
to the twenty-four and drink with D. At four AM

you must resist. People in San Francisco know this isn't
real pain. One has gold on his neck. Some of
them are drinking wine. I talk with mom about the
breakup. I write three letters to you in my head.
 J shits while we fuck. Her drawers are full of
strawberry condoms. V is in her room with Fleetwood Mac.
I take BART to Oakland. I talk to a face
inside the breeze. I smash my face into V's neck.
At three AM you must resist. Some sentences fall out
of M. Couples in the street piss me off then

make me happy. I drink until my hat falls off
and L laughs in a mirror. I walk through rain
to get clean and invisible. Things are the same as
they were two weeks ago. M knocks a champagne flute
onto the floor. All the women perch on one branch.
I serve them peas and carrots and some kind of
meat. I run to watch the twenty-two. I get punched
in the head walking down Church. L says I look
like myself. My bed is a petal in a glass
of vodka. I tell D it's coffee on my shirt

not blood. It's late. There are four of us left.
It's been two years. Money is balled up in my
pocket. I'm smashed after three drinks. Her face is an
ear that cannot record. Her ear lobe is wet. I
count twenty-six steps while V and I kiss. They have
office-sex. They have sex on a couch. Z kisses me
when I expect more beer. There's blood all over my
sheets in the morning. I lay on my bed and
sweat. We think about our lives for five seconds and
go on with our night. I'll get back to you

with some ideas. The playground is full of sleepy kids.
One of them hits the other in the face. I
barely pay attention. Every door is locked for their safety.
I give them piggybacks when they don't fight. D takes
off his shoes to hop the fence. I lock him
in a piss-filled room. I finish my paperwork and feel
okay. R stabs A with a pen. I tell him
drop the scissors and leave the room. A's little hand
squeezes my throat. We make plans to meet in Dolores.
I'm going to hate seeing you. The cat hair on

your pants never changes. E and I finish the gin.
B just wants to watch basketball and smoke his weed.
J walks into her empty room. I'm nervous about orientation.
I imagine you with the guy with glasses. My kids
are no longer my kids. I don't miss being on
the floor. J and I sleep in my empty room.
R walks onto the empty playground. It'd be great to
see you. I'd really like to talk. I have empty
emotions. I think of my life in two years. I'll
probably need gloves. I beat the shit out of my

steering wheel. The next phase of my life begins. A
woman eats a man made of dreams. I work in
a house. All of the doors in the house are
locked. I live in a dump with barely any light.
She lives in a cottage in Berkeley. I can't let
go of the things I write. I send you a
notebook with a girl on a train. I live in
a darker city. Sometimes it rains and I go for
a walk. I'm up late every night. I can hear
the neighbors breaking their plates. The ghost we spoke in

GHOST DREAM

We find a boring lake.

Some islands turn grayish and blink.

She tells me *hang sacks from trees* and I don't.

She asks me if I'm floating.

I point at a black and blue mark.

I think of college and wait.

DREAM CAPACITOR

When I can't sleep, I think of others washing their hands in a cold dark stream. A sound from the forest makes them raise their heads. They walk through an apartment with the lights off. They eat spoonfuls of ash and stare at the freeway. I meet them upstairs with nothing to say. They find their way back to the living room couch. They float down the hallway with a knife in one hand. They tell me *forget about trees* and *no hidden portals*. One of them has tar in the corners of her eyes. Her hair is draped across a pillow. She sends me an email about being afraid.

GHOST (12:17 PM)

In my dreams, I have the same problems. I hear the birds
outside at night. She waits by an unreachable lake. I can hear
wolves as they run through the underbrush. They have seams
attached to their ankles attached to something I read in college.
She sends me a text: *Sorry not tonite, Ben. See u soon.*

GHOST CHAPTER

I have no questions for anyone.

They want to be held by the neon light of an OPEN sign.

They fill their pockets with sand.

They wake up and look at a deer.

I lay the crumpled body next to the convenience store.

N puts a plastic medal around my neck.

I'm tangled in the branches.

Something wants me to fall asleep.

GHOST CHAPTER

D travels through a forest in my mind.

He's going to kill a monster I haven't thought of yet.

Another kid flips up his hood to avoid detection.

In my dreams, I have the same problems.

I hear the birds outside at night.

Vampires flood the meadows.

C waits by an unreachable lake.

D takes off his shoes to hop the fence.

I forget to lock up the knives.

LOST GHOST

The forest devours my car.

I tie a bandana around my head.

I walk through a whale carcass.

I unweave the braid that grows from my stomach.

It touches J's forehead as she sleeps.

My office clothes slip from my body.

My penis looks at a table.

Zombies flush the meadows. Vampires flush the meadows. I
think *green bunnies* as D goes in the PSR. I say *green bunnies* to
protect me from the silence we make. I take an escalator to
another level. I take huge leaps to get to a garage full of
weapons. I choose a samurai sword to do I don't know what.
People I know are riding black keys. One of them climbs the
face of a stone idol. Another posts pixelated photographs. A
huge brain controls the waterfall. I blow the doors open with
wind from my eyelid. Enemies flood the garage with
motorcycles. He takes his time filling the shells.

GHOST CHAPTER

Tomorrow is orientation.

I get nervous by an elevator.

We make plans to quit with a pill.

I hang around on someone else's couch.

I can see out a window to a lie.

The shadow team is on the other side.

D is sulking about two weeks.

E is never in my poems.

GHOST (2:37 AM)

I'm throwing grass on the heads of two old men.

The grass isn't special and I've chewed on it.

Our movie isn't being produced by anyone.

A woman sticks a knife into my palm.

I walk out onto the veranda.

My brains are dripping on a wood bench.

We spend too long talking and I get lonely.

I feel like sex with a blonde on television.

GHOST CHAPTER

They have office-sex. They have sex on a couch. Their genitals look like audience members without hats. I get so tired of the feeling. I lay on my bed and sweat. I wasn't expecting much from the procedure. J sends me a text. I arrive at the bar like one who can mimic. She looks at herself through a forest of hair. She grants me a dream about being a better person. I walk to C's portrait with a toothbrush.

FIRST GHOST

The day goes on too long, gets brittle and close. I sleep on my stomach and drift through the rain. My ticket passes through a machine and I wander to a map. I'm still in her room, but I'm not there. I don't know who sleeps on the other side. It takes a year to sketch the pain.

SAME GHOST

I can't eat anything that begins with C. I can't run faster than that guy in my brain. I don't feel like emailing V in Morocco. He's scoring weed and not eating lamb. D shows me sketches of the comic we'll never write. We drink *High Life* and listen songs we can't remember. E thinks things are over. I didn't know how to do it in a hotel. I put a wet rag over my head. I was breathing fast.

GHOST TRANSMITTER

The knowledge of my receivers grows dim.
I can only misquote what the voice tries to say.
I will probably never see it in the mirror.
I am finally caressed by a thought.

GHOST NODE

There are people to call and people who have breakdowns. They get up, get dressed, walk around the house. Some rooms are dark and someone passes by a window. I walk to the station and try not to look. A part of me waits on platforms. Another dissects the body with its teeth. It places the organs in separate aluminum trays. It tastes sea urchin and spits. The samples are done, are clean and bright and never. I put them in cold water. I give them a place to live.

GHOST COUPLE

I'm granted a dream of an unglowing girl. She stops to speak like a mirror in droves. The end of the silence means nothing to me. The machine at his desk writing his dark. I do my best to picture her face. She puts her face inside a bed. People call back in a murmur of time. The streets are filled with outlines coated in rain. I have to erase what I compress. I can't get to the end of the block. I turn around and hear a voice.

The *you* of the question was not the *what* of the machine.

—Ann Lauterbach

ACKNOWLEDGMENTS

Poems in this manuscript have been published in: *Beeswax Magazine* (thank you Laureen Shifley and John Peck), *Caketrain* (thank you Amanda Raczkowski and Joseph Reed), *Coconut* (thank you Bruce Covey), *Cookiebomb* (thank you Ryan Manning), *Elimae* (thank you Coop Renner), *H_NGM_N* (thank you Nate Pritts), *Lungfull* (thank you Brendan Lorber and Lauren Ireland), *Shampoo* (thank you Del Ray Cross), *Saltgrass* (thank you Julia Cohen), *W.A.C.* (thank you Gene Kwak) and *Washington Square* (thank you Laren McClung, Christine Malvasi, and Levi Rubeck). Parts of this manuscript also appear in *Collected Ghost*, a chapbook published in the H_NGM_N portable document format series which remains available for free at www.h-ngm-n.com.

Some of these poems appear differently in their previous places of publication.

Thank you Cathy Che, Sasha Fletcher and Paige Taggart for your guidance in the completion of this book and for your friendship.

Thank you Nate Pritts for supporting my work for many years.

Ben Mirov is the author of the chapbooks *Collected Ghost* (H_NGM_N, 2009) and *I is to Vorticism* (New Michigan Press, 2010). He is general editor of *pax americana*. He is also poetry editor of *LIT Magazine*. Sometimes he blogs at isaghost.blogspot.com.

CPSIA information can be obtained at www.ICGtesting.com
Printed in the USA
BVOW080343160413

318248BV00002B/8/P